Little Pebble™

All Kinds of Weather

Cold Weather

by Sally Lee

T0052240

PEBBLE
a capstone imprint

Little Pebble is published by Pebble
1710 Roe Crest Drive,
North Mankato, Minnesota 56003
www.capstonepub.com

Library of Congress Cataloging-in-Publication Data
Names: Lee, Sally, 1943– author.
Title: Cold weather : a 4D book / by Sally Lee.
Description: North Mankato, Minnesota : Capstone Press, [2018] |
Series: Little pebble. All kinds of weather | Audience: Ages 4–8.
Identifiers: LCCN 2018018356 (print) |
LCCN 2018019906 (ebook) | ISBN 9781977102010 (eBook PDF) |
ISBN 9781977101884 (hardcover) | ISBN 9781977101952 (pbk.)
Subjects: LCSH: Cold—Juvenile literature. | Freezes
(Meteorology)—Juvenile literature. | Earth temperature—Juvenile
literature. | Weather—Juvenile literature. | Winter—Juvenile
literature.
Classification: LCC QC981.8.A5 (ebook) |
LCC QC981.8.A5 L435 2018 (print) | DDC 551.5/253—dc23
LC record available at https://lccn.loc.gov/2018018356

Editorial Credits
Marissa Kirkman, editor; Bobbie Nuytten, designer;
Tracy Cummins, media researcher; Kris Wilfahrt, production
specialist

Photo Credits
Alamy: Kathy deWitt, 17; Getty Images: Hero Images, 5;
iStockphoto: skynesher, 7; Shutterstock: Alinute Silzeviciute, 21,
Kichigin, 19, Maria Sbytova, 15, mexrix, 13, Nepster, 11,
PH888, 1, polygraphus, Design Element, Standret, Cover,
Vadym Lavra, 9, wowomnom, 12.

Table of Contents

BRRRR 4

Why Is It Cold? 6

How Is the Weather? 12

Have Fun! 20

Glossary 22
Read More 23
Internet Sites 23
Critical Thinking Questions . . 24
Index 24

BRRRR

There is ice on the lake.

I can see my breath.

It is cold today.

Why Is It Cold?

Fall and winter are

the coldest seasons.

They have the shortest days.

The sun heats the earth.

Short days get less sunlight.

They are colder.

Earth tilts away from
the sun in winter.
The sun's rays spread out.
They are not as strong.

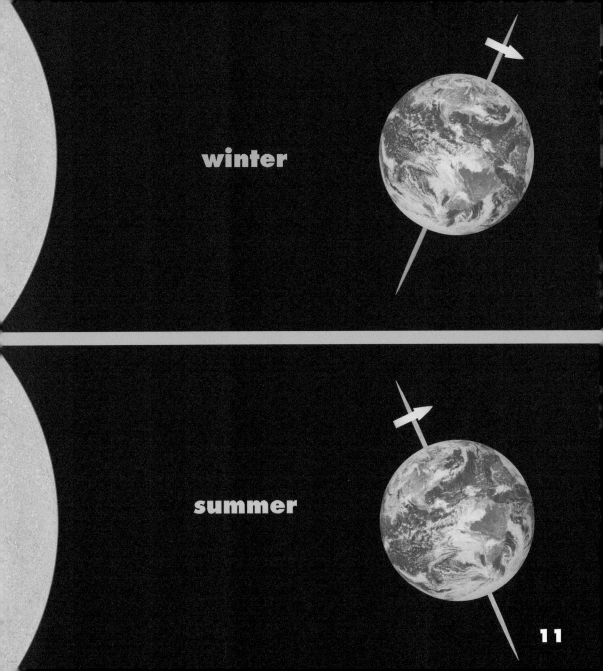

winter

summer

11

How Is the Weather?

How cold is it?

Will there be storms or snow?

Check the forecast to see.

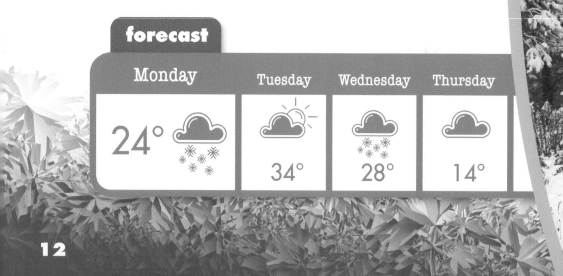

forecast			
Monday	**Tuesday**	**Wednesday**	**Thursday**
24°			
	34°	28°	14°

The temperature is low on cold days.
Wind and rain make it feel colder.

Rain drops can freeze
to make sleet.

Snow can fall on cold days.

Ice is frozen water.

It is slippery.

Be careful!

Don't slip!

Have Fun!

Cold days are fun!

Let's go ice skating.

Wheee!

Glossary

forecast—a report of future weather conditions

freeze—to become solid or icy at a very low temperature

frozen—being cold enough to turn from a liquid into a solid; ice is frozen water

ray—a line of light that beams out from something bright

season—one of the four parts of the year; winter, spring, summer, and fall are seasons

sleet—freezing rain

temperature—the measure of how hot or cold something is

tilt—an angle or lean; not straight

Read More

De Seve, Karen. *Little Kids First Big Book of Weather.* National Geographic Little Kids First Big Books. Washington, D.C.: National Geographic Kids, 2017.

Gleisner, Jenna Lee. *Weather in Fall.* Welcome, Fall! Mankato, Minn.: Child's World, 2017.

Sohn, Emily. *Experiments in Earth Science and Weather with Toys and Everyday Stuff.* Fun Science. North Mankato, Minn.: Capstone Press, 2016.

Internet Sites

Use FactHound to find Internet sites related to this book.

Visit www.facthound.com

Just type in 9781977101884 and go.

Super-cool stuff! Check out projects, games and lots more at **www.capstonekids.com**

Critical Thinking Questions

1. Why are fall and winter the coldest seasons?

2. What does the weather forecast tell us?

3. What can happen to rain drops on a cold day?

Index

earth, 8, 10
fall, 6
forecasts, 12
ice, 4, 18, 20
rain, 14, 16
sleet, 16

snow, 12, 16
storms, 12
sun, 10
temperature, 14
wind, 14
winter, 6, 10